Migrating Animals

Storks

Arthur Best

Cavendish Square

New York

Published in 2019 by Cavendish Square Publishing, LLC
243 5th Avenue, Suite 136, New York, NY 10016

Library of Congress Cataloging-in-Publication Data

Names: Best, B. J., 1976- author.
Title: Storks / Arthur Best.
Description: First edition. | New York : Cavendish Square, 2019. |
Series: Migrating animals | Audience: K to grade 2. | Includes index.
Identifiers: LCCN 2017059666 (print) | LCCN 2017060178 (ebook) | ISBN 9781502637222 (ebook) |
ISBN 9781502637215 (library bound) | ISBN 9781502637239 (pbk.) | ISBN 9781502637246 (6 pack)
Subjects: LCSH: Storks--Migration--Juvenile literature. | Animal migration--Juvenile literature.
Classification: LCC QL696.C535 (ebook) | LCC QL696.C535 B47 2019 (print) | DDC 598.3/4--dc23
LC record available at https://lccn.loc.gov/2017059666

Editorial Director: David McNamara
Copy Editor: Nathan Heidelberger
Associate Art Director: Amy Greenan
Designer: Megan Metté
Production Coordinator: Karol Szymczuk
Photo Research: J8 Media

The photographs in this book are used by permission and through the courtesy of: Cover Kotomiti Okuma/Shutterstock.com; p. 5 Zocha_K/iStock; p. 7 Andyworks/iStock; p. 9 Panoramic Images/Getty Images; p. 11 Freder/iStock; p. 13 bostb/iStock; p. 15 MyLoupe/Universal Images Group/Getty Images; p. 17 A_Lesik/Shutterstock.com; p. 19 Daneel85/iStock; p. 21 dmf87/iStock.

Printed in the United States of America

Contents

Storks are birds.

They are tall.

5

Storks have long wings.

They can fly far!

7

Storks live in a group.

The group is called a **flock**.

Storks build nests.

The nests are big!

11

It is spring.

Storks lay eggs.

The eggs are in the nest.

13

The eggs **hatch**!

New storks are called **chicks**.

15

The chicks grow up.

Now it is fall.

It gets cooler.

17

The storks **migrate**.

They fly a long way.

It will be warmer.

19

It is spring.

The storks migrate back.

They will lay new eggs!

21

New Words

chicks (CHIX) Baby birds.

flock (FLAHK) A group of birds.

hatch (HACH) When a baby bird comes out of its egg.

migrate (MY-grate) To travel far to live in a new place.

storks (STORKS) Tall birds.

Index

About the Author

Arthur Best lives in Wisconsin with his wife and son. He has written many other books for children. He has seen storks in Africa.

About BOOKWORMS

Bookworms help independent readers gain reading confidence through high-frequency words, simple sentences, and strong picture/text support. Each book explores a concept that helps children relate what they read to the world they live in.